D1523043

YOU CHOOSE

AN INTERACTIVE ADVENTURE

CAN YOU BECOME A POP STAR?

BY ALLISON LASSIEUR

CAPSTONE PRESS
a capstone imprint

Published by Capstone Press, an imprint of Capstone.
1710 Roe Crest Drive
North Mankato, Minnesota 56003
capstonepub.com

Library of Congress Cataloging-in-Publication Data
Names: Lassieur, Allison, author.
Title: Can you become a pop star? : an interactive adventure / by Allison Lassieur.
Description: North Mankato : Capstone Press, 2022. | Series: You choose: chasing
fame and fortune | Includes bibliographical references. |Audience: Ages 8-12 |
Audience: Grades 4-6 | Summary: "Do you dream of belting out a chart-topping single
on stage in front of thousands of people? Even with talent and determination, it's a
long, winding journey to the top. Chart your path to stardom, facing real-life choices as
you go. Some choices may lead to center stage, while others lead to disappointment or
redirection into another career field"— Provided by publisher.
Identifiers: LCCN 2021029692 (print) | LCCN 2021029693 (ebook) | ISBN
9781663958976 (hardcover) | ISBN 9781666323788 (paperback) | ISBN
9781666323795 (pdf)
Subjects: LCSH: Popular music—Vocational guidance—Juvenile literature.
Classification: LCC ML3795 .L254 2022 (print) | LCC ML3795 (ebook) | DDC
781.64023—dc23
LC record available at https://lccn.loc.gov/2021029692
LC ebook record available at https://lccn.loc.gov/2021029693

Editorial Credits
Editor: Mandy Robbins; Designer: Heidi Thompson; Media Researcher: Jo Miller;
Production Specialist: Tori Abraham

Photo Credits
Getty Images: Ryan McVay, 86, Terry Vine, 19; Shutterstock: BRAIN2HANDS, 75,
Christian Bertrand, 10, DFree, 107 (right), donatas1205, 70, dwphotos, 62, G-Stock
Studio, 48, Gorodenkoff, 37, i_am_zews, 51, LightField Studios, 43, Master1305, 26,
Monkey Business Images, 28, Nejron Photo, 72, Netfalls Remy Musser, Cover (right),
Rasstock, 91, Rawpixel.com, 68, 81, Razym, Cover (left), Ruslan Grumble, 55, Studio
Romantic, 98, yakub88, 107 (left)
Design Elements: Shutterstock: LeksusTuss, Nina_FOX, Southern Wind

All internet sites appearing in back matter were available and accurate when this book
was sent to press.

TABLE OF CONTENTS

MAKING IT BIG!

YOU have big dreams. You want the fame. You want the fortune. And you're willing to do whatever it takes to make your dreams come true. But it's never a straight shot to the top, especially in the highly competitive music industry. Find out if you have what it takes to find fame and fortune as a pop star.

• Turn the page.

The first chapter sets the scene. Then you choose which path to read. Follow the directions at the bottom of each page. The choices you make will change your outcome. After you finish one path, go back and read the others for more adventures.

• To begin your adventure, turn the page.

YOU CHOOSE
THE PATH YOU TAKE TO
POP STARDOM.

DO YOU HAVE
WHAT IT TAKES
TO BE A POP
SUPERSTAR?

These days it seems like everyone knows someone who wants to be a pop star. It could be the kid in choir or the friend who is the first to belt out karaoke tunes. It might even be you!

It's an impossible dream. Or is it? Plenty of ordinary people have shot to pop star fame.

• Turn the page.

Justin Bieber's fame started after his mom posted videos online of him singing at age 13. Billie Eilish shot to pop fame at age 14 when she uploaded her song "Ocean Eyes" to SoundCloud. Superstar Kelly Clarkson won the first season of *American Idol* in 2002. Taylor Swift got her start as an up-and-coming songwriter in Nashville. If they can do it, why not you?

But becoming a pop star takes more than a good voice and a few cool videos or live shows. The road to stardom can be long and hard, and very few people make it. Most who do share a few things in common.

A WILLINGNESS TO WORK HARD

It's easy to believe pop stars appear out of nowhere and become overnight successes. But most stars start small and work their way up. Working hard means playing for family and friends to get your name out. It's spending hours writing songs, taking music or voice lessons, or perfecting dance moves. It's convincing clubs to give you a chance and building a fan base with local performances. It means hours online maintaining and updating websites and keeping up with social media.

• Turn the page.

UNDERSTAND YOUR STRENGTHS AND WEAKNESSES

Being a pop star doesn't mean you're just good at singing. Some stars have a killer voice but aren't that great at performing live. Or they have great stage presence but an average voice. Others are fantastic songwriters, while others are better at dancing. Some pop stars are great at creating an image or a brand. While all pop stars must have a good voice, they also focus on what they're best at and use it to their advantage. When a singer capitalizes on strengths, it can turn into stardom.

HAVE A SUPPORT SYSTEM

No one makes it to stardom on their own. Every successful pop star can look back at people who helped them become who they are.

Maybe it was family members who believed in them. It might have been friends or a teacher who helped them achieve their dream. Once they hit the big time, pop stars still need support. They have huge teams that help with songwriting, booking concerts and photo shoots, and much more.

HAVE NO FEAR OF PROMOTING YOURSELF

To make it to stardom, you must get people in the music business to notice you. Every pop superstar had a moment when a music industry pro saw them. Even if their story sounds like a one-in-a-million accident, it probably wasn't. They knew how to show their talent in the right place to get noticed.

• Turn the page.

There are lots of ways to promote yourself. Find places where other musicians hang out. Introduce yourself and ask questions. Offer to perform at celebrations or local events. Watch for talent shows, open mic nights, and tryout opportunities.

PERSISTENCE

Every superstar wanted to give up at some point. Persistence kept them going. Almost no one makes it big right out of the gate. So what if your first concert bombed? Who cares if your first video only got three views—all from your mom. That doesn't mean it's time to give up. The path to pop stardom is filled with mistakes and rejections. The most successful artists learn to power through setbacks.

If you have all of these qualities, you've got a chance to become a pop star. There are a lot of paths to pop stardom for you to explore:

- To try to use the power of social media to become a pop star, turn to page 17.
- To join a band, play local venues, and build an in-person fan base that will propel you to stardom, turn to page 45.
- To focus on shooting to fame by auditioning for a reality TV talent show, turn to page 77.

VIRAL POP STARDOM

Lately, you've been spending hours on your laptop. You listen to new music and watch videos. When you're not online, you practice music on your electric keyboard. It's not top-of-the-line, but it has features like percussion and a record function. After weeks of practice, you've written a song that you think is good enough to record. All you have is a smartphone and a few free music apps. But according to the internet, that's more than enough to make a good music video.

• Turn the page.

But when you start making your music video, it's much harder than it looks online. The first takes sound terrible, and the lighting is too dark. After several hours, you finally get a video you're happy with. With a deep breath, you upload it to your social media accounts, crossing your fingers that it will go viral.

Then you wait. And wait. A few likes and comments trickle in. Some of them criticize the sound quality and the shaky video. Friends and family love it and ask for more. After a few days, the views stop, and everyone forgets the song you worked so hard on.

It's discouraging, but it makes you more determined to get your music out there. You consider buying some better recording equipment. But you'd have to spend all your birthday money on it. Besides, you love the rawness of the phone video and don't want to lose that.

- To keep the authentic sound and make more videos like the first, turn to page 20.
- To invest in some equipment before recording a new song, turn to page 29.

19

You set up a personal music channel. Creating content is a lot harder and more time consuming than you expected, though. You plan to upload a new video every few weeks. But it's a struggle to keep up the pace of writing, practicing, and recording music. It feels worth it when every upload gets a few more shares. It's mostly friends and family, but you'll take it.

After several months of work, the likes start dropping off. Many comments compliment your music. Others complain about the poor quality of the videos. The people commenting don't get what you're trying to do with your raw, edgy look and sound. Maybe if you can attract new listeners, more people will appreciate your style.

One day you get a break. A music podcaster texts you. She's planning a podcast on local musicians and wants to interview you!

This is your opportunity to explain your style. The show airs a week later. Your channel gets hundreds of new followers. It's exciting to finally connect with people who understand your style. You're even more eager to finish your next video. You're sure this one will go viral.

The podcaster thinks you should apply for a copyright on your songs. It would prove they're legally yours. But the fact that you've posted these videos proves you own the songs, so you don't see the need. The new video gets some positive comments but few new followers. So does the next one, and the one after that. Discouragement sets in. You've been at this for months, and all you have to show for it are a handful of videos. You still love music, but you begin questioning whether it's worth the time and energy to try to become a star.

- To continue chasing the dream, turn to page 22.
- To quit, turn to page 27.

Maybe a new online look is what you need to get noticed. You redesign your channel. You even build a website. The results look great.

The day your new sites goes live, hundreds of angry texts blow up your social media. People are saying you stole someone's song. You click on a link to a video from a singer you've never heard of. You're horrified as he performs one of your songs! He's playing guitar instead of a keyboard. The video quality is much better. But it's definitely your music.

You email and text him but he ignores and blocks you. He deletes your comments on his website and music channel. The podcaster who interviewed you finds out what's going on and offers to put you in touch with a lawyer.

- To fight this thief, go to page 23.
- To ignore it and move on, turn to page 25.

The lawyer doesn't have good news. The most she can do is send a cease and desist letter, demanding that he take down the video. She can also report him to his web-hosting company. They could issue a notice to remove the video. But these companies don't always enforce the notices. If they don't, nothing will happen to him.

You could also sue him for stealing your song. But you would have to prove that he heard your song and saw your video before he made his.

You ask the lawyer to send the cease and desist letter. Hopefully, it will scare the thief into taking down the video.

Instead, he accuses you of copying him! He has more followers than you, and they believe him.

• Turn the page.

People post insults and threats on your social media. It takes several weeks before the musician finally takes down the video. You can't take much more of this. Bitter and exhausted, you shut down your channel. Maybe making music for yourself and your friends is better than pop stardom.

--- THE END ---

To follow another path, turn to page 15.
To learn more about becoming a pop star, turn to page 103.

You're bummed, but don't want to start a legal battle. And you're not going to let one jerk ruin your dream. Going forward, you'll protect your music. You register your songs with the United States Copyright Office. This process involves making copies of every song to prove when you created them. You create an online alert system that tells you if anyone sends your music to anyone else. Then you can ask the website hosting company to issue a takedown notice to anyone who does.

Slowly, you rebuild your online popularity. After a year of hard work, you have a decent following. You still shoot all your videos with your phone. It's become your look. You are invited to perform at a small music festival. That show leads to a regular gig at a downtown coffeehouse.

• Turn the page.

It's a long way from the red carpet, but you're making money! You can honestly call yourself a professional musician.

--- THE END ---

To follow another path, turn to page 15.
To learn more about becoming a pop star, turn to page 103.

A few days after you take down your channel, you get a text from a friend. She's starting a band and looking for a keyboard player. You've never wanted to be in a band. You wanted to do your own thing. She won't take no for an answer, though. You figure you've got nothing to lose by meeting with them.

You're nervous, but they make you feel welcome. After a couple hours, you feel like you've been part of the group forever. They're amazing musicians too. When you start playing together, something magical happens. They feel it too. They ask you to join the band, and you say yes.

For the first time in a while you're excited about music again. It's a relief not to be doing everything by yourself.

• Turn the page.

Everyone pitches in to write music, make videos, and keep up with social media. You may never become pop stars, but you're making music with people you like. That's enough for you.

--- THE END ---

To follow another path, turn to page 15.
To learn more about becoming a pop star, turn to page 103.

You spend a few hundred dollars on good equipment, and it makes a big difference. The sound is better. The videos look professional.

Several months go by, and you've finished three new covers of your favorite pop songs. They're your best work, but for some reason you're not getting many new views and likes.

You need to do something to increase your following. You prefer to do covers, but maybe you could get more attention if you write some original songs. Or maybe you should start a blog. You could open up about who you are as a musician. Your fans could follow along as you document your musical journey.

- To write your own music, turn to page 30.
- To start blogging about your musical journey, turn to page 38.

The internet is overrun with "how to write a hit song" websites and videos. They all have different advice. Some give tips on how to be original. Others explain basic musical terms like chord progressions and major versus minor keys.

For weeks you struggle to write something good, using the built-in beats and melodies from your keyboard. You even try free music apps on your phone. Finally you have a song you're happy with. When you upload it to your channel, no one likes it. All that work for nothing. Or was it? The more you listen to your song, the more you hear things that you don't like. It's hard to admit, but maybe it wasn't as good as you first thought. You've learned a lot about music and songwriting. The next one will probably be better. Or should you just stick with covers?

- To decide to go back to covers, go to page 31.
- To try writing more songs, turn to page 33.

You go back to singing covers. After a few months of hard work, the views on your videos climb into the thousands. The more popular the band you cover, the more traffic your channel gets. You begin selling memberships to your channel. You also sell T-shirts from the bands and singers you cover. Soon you're making several hundred dollars every month. If this keeps up you might just be able to make a living as a full-time online musician! Your dream of pop stardom is so close you can feel it.

Then a cease and desist letter appears in your inbox. It's from the legal team of one of the bands whose images appear on your merch. Apparently it is illegal to make money off of another artist's image and likeness.

• Turn the page.

The letter says that you have acted in an illegal manner. The band will take you to court if you don't take down the videos and stop selling the merch. You could lose more money than you've ever made online.

You take down all the videos and remove the merch from your store. The experience scares you! You take down other videos and stop selling merch from the most popular bands you've covered. Hundreds of memberships get canceled. You're barely making any money now. You still record and upload covers, but your heart isn't in it anymore. After a while, you shut down your channel for good.

--- THE END ---

To follow another path, turn to page 15.
To learn more about becoming a pop star, turn to page 103.

Your first songs are pretty terrible, but you keep writing. You decide to shut down your channel for a while and focus on learning about songwriting. You sign up for online songwriting classes. You watch a lot of how-to videos to learn more about making your own videos. After a year working on your skills, you reboot your channel and start making videos again.

While online, you stumble across a site advertising a video competition. A little more digging comes up with quite a few of these contests. The prizes range from cash to new instruments to meeting with a producer. Winning would definitely help relaunch your online music career. But thousands of musicians enter these contests. It would take some work to create an entry video. The chances of you winning one are pretty small.

- To focus on rebuilding your channel and website, turn to page 34.
- To put off relaunching your site to enter contests, turn to page 36.

You finish rebuilding your website. You record new videos and update all your social media. You use email lists and social media to advertise. That brings more traffic to your channel.

To your delight, the first video you drop goes viral! So does the second. You build a huge new following, with thousands of views on every video and tens of thousands of streams for each song.

Your work catches the attention of several well-known music websites and podcasters. They request interviews and appearances. Things are moving fast! You hire a manager to help you keep up. She books interviews and arranges an online acoustic concert.

You're making a lot of money from your music, but no one outside the internet knows who you are. That changes in a single day.

A superstar singer asks to work with you on a song for his new album. The album is nominated for several Video Music Awards (VMAs). Unbelievably, you find yourself walking the red carpet. Flashbulbs pop in your face and reporters shout your name. It's your pop stardom dream come true!

--- THE END ---

To follow another path, turn to page 15.
To learn more about becoming a pop star, turn to page 103.

You drop everything to make a killer video. After a busy few days, it's finished. You enter it in a dozen different contests. You're disappointed but not surprised when the rejections start coming back. However, one email has great news—your video won a contest! The prize is a meeting with the public relations team of an independent music label.

The label pays for your flight and a room at a fancy hotel. You meet with the staff. They loved your video! They have suggestions for how you can build your brand. They post your videos on their industry website. This is great exposure. You're disappointed that they don't offer to sign you. You hope these insider connections will be useful. Now it's time to relaunch your online career on the path to stardom.

--- THE END ---

To follow another path, turn to page 15.
To learn more about becoming a pop star, turn to page 103.

It feels good to write about your struggles to break into the industry. To your surprise, a lot of people feel the same way. Like you, they're musicians just starting out. Most of them focus on cover songs as well, which makes you feel good. You exchange tips and advice. You share horror stories about the experience of trying to be an internet pop star. Before you know it, your blog site is home for a whole community of musicians.

You're having fun, but writing new blog content and keeping up your social media takes all your time. You rarely manage to get new videos shot and uploaded. You can't keep it all up for much longer.

- To decide to focus on music, go to page 39.
- To focus just on your social media work, turn to page 41.

Without the pressure of writing blog content, you shoot several new videos. Some are covers, but a few are original songs. At this point, you're not thinking about anything going viral. You just want your music out there for people to enjoy.

On a whim, you submit a video to an online station. It hosts a livestream concert series. A couple of months later they invite you to perform. You've never done a live online performance before. You've only ever uploaded videos. You have a new song in the works. You haven't made a video for it yet. So you decide to upload it to Spotify and perform it during the live show.

As soon as you play the new song, traffic to your site jumps. By the end of the concert, the song has thousands of streams. The concert producer is so pleased, he invites you back.

• Turn the page.

Over the next year, you become a regular performer on the series. You get almost a million new fans to your channel. Your videos and songs get hundreds of thousands of downloads and streams. They make you enough money to live on. You are now a full-time musician. You might never win a Grammy, but you're officially an online indie pop sensation.

--- THE END ---

To follow another path, turn to page 15.
To learn more about becoming a pop star, turn to page 103.

There's always something to talk about in the music world. People seem to like what you have to say. You expand the blog by starting your own music podcast. On it, you review music sites and offer tips for new musicians. Slowly, you build an audience who pay a yearly subscription.

One day, a retired music producer hears one of your podcasts. He is impressed and offers to come on your podcast. He was very successful, and his name is still widely known in the industry. You jump at the chance to meet him.

The interview wins you millions of downloads and streams! His appearance gets the attention of other industry professionals. They agree to come on your podcast too. The podcast becomes so successful that you expand and hire a staff. You've earned a reputation as an honest, respected music broadcaster.

• Turn the page.

It crosses your mind to take advantage of your new connections to promote your own music. But you've seen and heard enough about the gritty inside workings of the music industry. You don't think you'd ever cut it as a pop star. You don't mind, though. You're happy with the music career you've built.

--- THE END ---

To follow another path, turn to page 15.
To learn more about becoming a pop star, turn to page 103.

POUNDING THE PAVEMENT TO STARDOM

When you were growing up, any room with more than two people in it was your stage. You belted out radio pop tunes in kindergarten You begged for guitar lessons and piano lessons. In high school, you sang in the choir and got the lead in every school musical. You were voted "Most Likely to Be a Star" in your high school yearbook.

• Turn the page.

But as you grew older, the fame and glory you dreamed of didn't happen. You had quit college to join a band. Your group had one viral video and a single summer-festival tour. After that, the band broke up. You're not giving up on your dream yet, but you're not sure what to do next.

One day a friend in the music business mentions that a band he knows is looking for a lead singer. He also gives you the contact information of an A&R rep at an up-and-coming record label. A&R reps are basically talent scouts. She might be able to help you launch a solo career.

- To meet with the band, go to page 47.
- To send a message to the A&R rep, turn to page 67.

The band is fairly well known in the area. They give you five of their songs to learn. You spend the next two weeks practicing them. You even learn a few more songs from their website. You're a little worried that their sound doesn't match yours. They're more techno party rock, and you're more of a folk-pop singer. But you're determined to give it a try. You know you can do it.

You're a bundle of nerves on audition day. You've chosen an outfit that's edgy but not too weird. The band members are friendly. They're impressed with your touring experience. They're good musicians too. You nail every song they asked for. When they start playing one of their early songs, you shock them by knowing it too.

• Turn the page.

The next hour flies by in a free-flowing jam session. By the time it's over you have the job if you want it. But you're not sure if you want to sing their music or keep working on your own.

- To turn them down, go to page 49.
- To join the band, turn to page 54.

If you're going to go for pop star fame, you're going to do it with your own music. You love performing live in small places. Starting with short weekend tours sounds like a good idea. A weekend tour will take you to towns that are close enough to drive to in one weekend. But they're far enough away that few people have heard of you there.

Scheduling gigs is time-consuming work, especially for an unknown solo act. First you research places to perform in nearby towns. You contact each one through text, email, or by calling them. You book gigs in coffee shops, hotels, small theaters, and even church basements. You have to bring your own equipment. You send flyers to local businesses and post announcements all over social media.

• Turn the page.

The first few gigs are disappointing. The crowds are small. Sometimes you play to an almost-empty room. You don't get paid much, if you get paid at all. It takes several months, but you slowly build a following. You become a regular act at a couple of clubs. Since you're bringing in more people, the clubs start paying you more. This helps convince other places in larger areas to book you.

After a year, you've got a solid following. You're making money, but it's not enough to live on. You need to get a regular job. The only one you can find in your town requires you to work weekend hours. That means you'll have to give up playing on the weekends. You mention your dilemma to the owner of the biggest club you play, and she offers you a job as a talent buyer. It would be a great opportunity!

Your job would be to hire musical acts for the club. But it would also mean moving to a new town several hours from home. You're not sure you're up to a big life change.

- To keep the job in your hometown, turn to page 52.
- To accept the club owner's offer, turn to page 53.

You take the job in your hometown, pack away your tour equipment, and settle back into regular life. But you can't completely give up music. You form a group with some musicians you know. Everyone has jobs and family responsibilities, but you manage to get together now and then to write songs and jam. You play the occasional graduation party or family gathering. You gave chasing your dream a shot, and the life you have now is alright. You wouldn't change a thing.

--- THE END ---

To follow another path, turn to page 15.
To learn more about becoming a pop star, turn to page 103.

It's hard to leave home, but it's a dream job. You spend your days looking for talent. You cut deals with booking agents and finalize details for each performance. Your knack for spotting new talent is obvious. You help the club build a hot reputation in the music world.

A couple of years go by. One of the unknown bands you discovered makes it big. Your club gets instant celebrity status. Big-name music labels can't wait to book their bands with you. Up-and-coming acts from all over the country beg to play there. When you dreamed of making it in the music business you didn't think it would be like this. But you love how it turned out.

--- THE END ---

To follow another path, turn to page 15.
To learn more about becoming a pop star, turn to page 103.

The first few weeks of rehearsals feel great. You don't love the music style, but you're learning a lot.

The band shoots a few videos for their YouTube channel. The first video with you as the band's new lead singer gets a huge number of views. The second does even better. Views jump into the tens of thousands. One video goes viral for a few days when a famous actor shares it on his social media. Everyone in the band is thrilled. They give you credit for their newfound popularity.

The band needs to carefully choose its next step. Some members want to build on this new popularity by making a promotional recording called a demo. A well-made demo could help get the band a record deal.

Others insist on doing a big multistate tour while the songs and video are still hot. They argue that building a strong fan base will attract the attention of the music industry.

- To vote to make a demo, turn to page 56.
- To attempt a big tour, turn to page 65.

A professional studio demo can cost thousands of dollars. So the band decides on a do-it-yourself recording. At first, you think the band will simply get together and play songs while someone records them. You soon learn that there's a lot more to it than that. First you record each instrument and the vocals separately. From there, the tracks are put into a sound mixing program to be mixed, or blended together. Then the volume and tone are adjusted so that it all fits together. Finally, special effects like echoes are added to get the band's techno party rock sound.

It takes a couple of weeks to make the demo, but the end result sounds great. The band sends it to agents, music promoters, and talent buyers. These music professionals are all involved in booking and promoting acts for clubs and festivals.

The head of a small label you've never heard of contacts the band. This could be your chance at a record deal. You also hear from the talent buyer of a famous summer music festival. He invites the band to its side-stage lineup. You're a live-performance musician. You want to do the festival. The other band members think the fastest way to stardom is through a record deal.

- To go along with your bandmates and meet with the record label, turn to page 58.
- To convince your bandmates to play the festival, turn to page 63.

The band gets a free trip to Los Angeles. You spend several whirlwind days meeting with the label representatives. They treat you to expensive restaurants. They show you their high-tech recording studio and arrange meetings with their publicists and stylists. They even take the band to Disneyland. The label reps promise they can make you all pop superstars. It feels like a dream that you don't ever want to wake up from.

On the last night you're in town, the label throws a party. There they offer you a record contract! The rest of the band is eager to sign. You're not sure, though. You've heard that some record deals can turn out badly for musicians. But everyone has been so nice and supportive, it's hard to believe they'd try to cheat you.

- To sign the contract, go to page 59.
- To go home without signing, turn to page 61.

You're going to be a pop star sensation! The label loans, or advances, the band $500,000. That money pays for a publicist, a manager, and travel, tour, and studio costs. The contract says the band must make five albums. You get to work on the first, or debut, album right away. Six months and a lot of hard work later, the album is done. The publicist books the band on TV talk shows and concerts to packed audiences. Everywhere you go, you're treated like a star. You ride around in limos. Assistants cater to your every whim.

But the album doesn't do as well as everyone had hoped. And it turns out you signed what is known as a 360 contract. The contract says the label owns everything—your music, your videos, your streams, your merch, all tour earnings. You get a percentage of all those sales, but that goes to paying back the $500,000 advance money.

• Turn the page.

If a record doesn't sell, the band still has to repay the money. The label threatens to drop the band if the next album isn't a hit.

The second album makes millions of dollars, but the label gets almost all of it. For the next three years, the band records albums, shoots videos, and tours. It's amazing to sing in front of thousands of fans, sign autographs, and give interviews. But behind the scenes, you're broke and exhausted.

Then your label signs a new band with a sound like yours. The label doesn't want you competing with their new hitmaker. They never even release your last two albums. Appearances and tours get canceled. The label drops you. Your moment is over. You had the fame, but you never got the fortune.

--- THE END ---

To follow another path, turn to page 15.
To learn more about becoming a pop star, turn to page 103.

You won't sign a contract without having a lawyer look at it. Back home, the band hires a lawyer to do just that. She tells you the contract is a 360 deal. That means the label would own the rights to all of your music, merch, tour tickets—everything. She tries to get you a better contract with the label, but they refuse. It's a bitter blow to be that close to stardom and not get it. But the band agrees that it's better to have control than lose all the rights to their music.

You get back to the normal life of rehearsing and recording. One day you casually share your folk-pop music with the band. To your surprise, they love the sound. Together, you make several songs with a new techno folk-pop fusion sound that your fans love. Your music channel hits a million views. The streams are off the charts!

• Turn the page.

The band hires a booking agent and a manager. Local concerts sell out, and so do places in nearby cities. You're becoming a real pop star, and the best part is that your music is all yours.

--- THE END ---

To follow another path, turn to page 15.
To learn more about becoming a pop star, turn to page 103.

You convince your bandmates that playing a world-famous festival is more exciting than meeting with a label. But behind the scenes, it's a dirty, expensive job. Once you pay for travel to the festival, food, and gas, you're nearly broke. The festival doesn't pay unknown bands very much. You set up a merch table and hope to break even.

Every band plays several sets over the festival weekend. Your first performance brings down the house! By the time your third set is over, you've become the buzz of the festival. A great review appears on the cover of the festival's daily newspaper. The rest of the weekend flashes by like a crazy dream. A local TV station livestreams an interview with the band. A national magazine includes the band on their "New Acts to Watch" festival website.

• Turn the page.

You record a couple of live songs in the on-site recording studio that get played around the country. You even end up in an all-night jam session with a rock star you've admired all your life.

By the time you pack up, the band has scheduled meetings with three record labels. You also get an invitation to open for your rock-star idol when his tour comes to your town. Only days ago you were nobody, and now you're an up-and-coming pop star.

--- THE END ---

To follow another path, turn to page 15.
To learn more about becoming a pop star, turn to page 103.

You're the only member of the band who's ever been on a tour, so you explain how to plan one. Someone has to contact the locations and schedule shows. The towns you play in should only be a couple hours' drive apart, so you're not on the road for days between shows. In cities where no one knows the band, advertising is a must. Flyers, emails, social media announcements, and an online press kit with videos and photos can build excitement for the show. Someone has to book hotels too.

You all get to work planning the tour. Finally, everything is done. The band hits the road, excited and nervous. But no one shows up to your first show, or the second. It turns out the bandmate responsible for advertising only sent out a few tweets and some posts to social media. It wasn't nearly enough.

• Turn the page.

In a panic, you try to fix this with a flood of online announcements, invitations, and videos. You drive all night to get to the next town in time to put up posters before the show. A few people show up, but not enough. By now everyone's nerves are on edge. Band members start arguing. The next venue cancels your appearance. The tour was a failure. The band drives home in silence and breaks up soon after.

--- THE END ---

To follow another path, turn to page 15.
To learn more about becoming a pop star, turn to page 103.

The A&R rep is excited you're now a solo act. She loves your sound but suggests that you'd be more popular if you changed your style. You don't think much of it and eagerly sign a two-album record deal. It's a new label, so they can't afford to give you advance money for promotion and recording. Instead, they'll handle it all for you. The rep gets you a manager to lead you through the process. You're going to be a pop star!

Things start to get strange as work on your first, or debut, album starts. Your new manager encourages you to change your hairstyle. He hires a stylist to help you choose new clothes for videos. The label has songwriters write songs for you. What they come up with isn't anything like the songs you write. Your manager explains that you only have one chance to hit the big time.

• Turn the page.

For now, you have to do what the label says.

Once you're a star, you can make your own music.

- To listen to your manager, go to page 69.
- To stay true to your music and who you are, turn to page 71.

They're the professionals, so you trust them. You give them all your social media accounts, your fan email list, and copies of the songs you've written. The label ramps up the marketing. They send you on a press tour of radio stations and music podcasts. They fill social media with ads and teaser videos. You do daytime talk show concerts. It pays off when your album debuts in the Top 10!

After that, things really kick into high gear. A video from the album wins several awards. One song becomes the most-streamed song of the year. You win a Grammy for Best New Artist!

All of the fame is exciting, but you feel like you're selling an image and not who you really are. After you release your second album, you make a deal for a better contract.

• Turn the page.

From now on you'll own your music, and you can make music you want to play. Your new fans might not be expecting your real sound. But at least you'll be true to yourself.

--- THE END ---

To follow another path, turn to page 15.
To learn more about becoming a pop star, turn to page 103.

You spend months feeling guilty and nervous at the idea that you blew your only chance at pop stardom. The two things that help clear your head are writing songs and playing online video games.

For fun, you write a couple of songs inspired by your favorite game and make a video complete with costumes and props. You're shocked when the video goes viral on gamer sites and social media! You had no idea there was such a huge audience for music based on video games. You also discover a gaming platform that has music channels where musicians host livestream concerts. This opens up a whole new place where your music could be successful.

- To make more videos, turn to page 72.
- To start a livestream concert channel, turn to page 74.

You loved making the first gamer video, so you decide to stick to that. Each video is more detailed than the last, with costumes and makeup. You even hire a professional videographer. You find out that video game music is a multibillion-dollar industry.

One day you get an email from a game developer. They're interested in using one of your songs in their new game. They offer you a lot of money and a fair contract. You agree!

The game is a monster hit! Your song goes viral everywhere. You're invited to be the main performer at one of the biggest science-fiction conventions in the country. There, you're treated like a rock star. You give interviews and sign autographs. A&R reps from two labels offer you contracts. It might not be the route to pop stardom that you imagined, but you love it!

--- THE END ---

To follow another path, turn to page 15.
To learn more about becoming a pop star, turn to page 103.

You host a livestream concert every week. Slowly you build a fan base. At first you do covers of popular game music. Little by little, you add original songs. It's great how this platform lets you chat with your viewers while you perform. You open subscriptions to your concert channel and start making money.

You connect with other musicians in the video game industry and invite them to play with you. After a year, your concerts bring in thousands of fans. You're making more money than you ever imagined. You may not be a huge star, but this kind of pop stardom is just right for you.

--- THE END ---

To follow another path, turn to page 15.
To learn more about becoming a pop star, turn to page 103.

REALITY TV
STARDOM

Growing up, your favorite television shows were reality talent competitions. You loved rooting for your favorite contestants. You wore out not one, but two, karaoke machines practicing and performing their songs. When you were old enough, you'd do whatever it took to be on one of these shows.

You're still chasing your pop star dream. You've been in a band for the last five years, but stardom hasn't happened.

• Turn the page.

The late nights lugging equipment in and out of dirty clubs is wearing you out. You're starting to accept that you may never be a pop star.

Late one night, you check your email and find a message from the producer of a national TV talent show. It's an invitation to audition as a singer for the show! It's too bad this show only accepts solo acts. The auditions are in a month. That gives you plenty of time to practice and prepare. But you'd need to take some time off from the band to focus on preparing for your audition. You're not sure the rest of the band would understand.

When you get to rehearsal the next day, your bandmates tell you that a brand new reality TV talent show has been announced. They're auditioning groups for a "battle of the bands" style of contest for their first season.

The bad news is that auditions for this show are in a big city a day's drive away. And they're also on the same weekend as the other one.

You don't say anything about the solo audition. Your bandmates discuss whether to spend the time and energy to prepare for the contest. They finally agree to go for it. Now you've got a choice to make. Do you stick with the band, or do you leave to try for a solo career?

- To audition with your bandmates, turn to page 80.
- To audition as a solo act, turn to page 88.

You've been with the band this far. You're going to stick with them. For the next month, your life is nothing but rehearsals, songwriting, and preparing for the big audition. Finally, it's time to hit the road. The band loads up and heads out. After an exhausting 10-hour drive, you arrive at the arena around dawn. Huge crowds have already lined up. When you finally get to the check-in table, you fill out a stack of paperwork. Then workers give you a number.

You're shaking from nerves and excitement. You're led to a huge holding room where everyone waits their turn. Camera crews wander through the crowds, shooting scenes for the show. By late afternoon, you're moved into another holding room full of bands waiting their turn. You had no idea the process would take this long.

The band has a gig tomorrow, and most of your bandmates are tired of waiting around. If you don't leave soon, you'll never make it home in time to get some sleep before your show.

- To leave the audition and return home, turn to page 82.
- To stay, turn to page 87.

Disappointed, you leave. It feels like giving up a dream. But you're not going to risk missing your show. You don't want the band to get a reputation for not showing up for paid performances.

The concert goes well. There's a lot of good energy in the room. It makes leaving the audition a little easier to bear. Between sets, a man and a woman approach you. They're producers of the reality show you backed out of earlier. They're looking for local talent and saw the band's videos online. They love your sound and invite you to travel to the celebrity judge round of auditions in Los Angeles! Of course you say yes. They explain that they'll be in touch after the audition tour is over in a few weeks.

It's unbelievable! The band immediately begins work on fresh songs, upgrading equipment, and even more practice.

The producers send you lots of forms. You have to sign an agreement not to tell anyone that you're going to be on the show. They explain that you should arrive at the audition with all your costumes, makeup, and equipment ready to go.

Months go by, and you don't hear anything. Maybe the show doesn't want you after all. Finally, one day the email arrives. Excitement hits you all over again. Some of your bandmates aren't as thrilled. They're angry that the producers took so long to get back to you. They don't trust the show to treat you right. You see where they're coming from, but you don't want to give up your dream. Part of you wants to convince them this is your best chance at stardom.

- To decline the invitation, turn to page 84.
- To convince them to go to Los Angeles, turn to page 85.

Even though you know it was the best decision, it makes you angry that your dreams of stardom have been crushed. Your bandmates say that it's almost impossible to win shows like this. And there's no guarantee of stardom even if you do win. You're too disappointed to listen to them. The fighting gets intense. The band breaks up, leaving your pop star dreams in the dust.

--- THE END ---

To follow another path, turn to page 15.
To learn more about becoming a pop star, turn to page 103.

It takes a lot of convincing, but the band finally agrees to go for it. You're going to be on TV! The show pays for your plane tickets and hotel in Los Angeles. You're so excited to be performing in front of the celebrity judges. The judges have to vote yes for you to make it on to the live show.

Like before, the contestants go into a holding area to wait their turn. It's busy and loud, with acts singing, playing, and practicing all around. Camera crews film everything. Your band gives several interviews as the day wears on. Finally, you're onstage with the celebrity judges. Your heart pounds as you quickly set up. It's unreal that you're actually here. After some friendly introductions, you begin.

• Turn the page.

When you're done, the judges thank you, and that's it. The cameras turn to the next contestant. You blew it. Your dreams of reality TV stardom are over.

--- THE END ---

To follow another path, turn to page 15.
To learn more about becoming a pop star, turn to page 103.

After more sitting around, they finally call your number. The band quickly sets up in front of a table where several producers sit. You only have 90 seconds to impress them. You all take a deep breath and start. Once you've finished, they explain that they don't pick the acts that move forward today. After the audition tour is over, the producers go back to Los Angeles. They'll spend weeks reviewing all the audition tapes. It will be months before you hear anything.

Back home, the owner of the club you were supposed to play is furious. He fires the band. Soon after, you get a short rejection email thanking the band for participating in the auditions. Now you feel like a double failure.

--- THE END ---

To follow another path, turn to page 15.
To learn more about becoming a pop star, turn to page 103.

The band isn't happy, but they wish you luck. Then they quickly hire a new lead singer. There's no turning back now.

You spend the next month perfecting several songs. You choose your wardrobe and watch every episode of the show. You fill out lots of online paperwork. Some forms ask for personal details about your life and why you want to win the competition.

When you arrive, thousands of people are waiting to sign in. You feel proud walking to the front of the line and showing your invitation. You're instantly taken inside to a large room. There, 50 or 60 singers are already waiting. The producers explain that you've skipped the first round and will audition in Round 2.

After hours of waiting, you and three other
singers are shown into another room that's
curtained off into sections. One by one, they sing
the first verse and chorus of the song they chose.
When it's your turn, you belt out your song the
best you can. The producers dismiss the other
three and ask you to sing another song. The song
you choose could change your life.

- To sing one of your original folk-inspired songs, turn to
page 90.
- To lean toward a proven pop song, turn to page 94.

This is your shot to get your own music heard. You let everything go and sing from the heart. When it's done, one producer looks amazed. The rest don't. When they face you with blank expressions, you know. They explain that you were great, but they've already chosen other singers with a similar sound. It's hard to hold back the tears as you leave. The producer who liked you runs out and hands you a business card. She tells you to contact her after the audition tour is over. She has contacts who would love to hear you.

A few months go by, and your life gets back to normal. One day you run across her card and figure you don't have anything to lose. You leave her a message. To your amazement, she replies immediately. She tells you an older pop star is working on his comeback album, and he's looking for backup singers. She offers to put you in touch with him.

- To decline the offer, go to page 91.
- To agree to the offer, turn to page 92.

As tempting as the offer is, you want to be a lead solo act. She understands, and tells you how talented you are. You thank her for her interest and support. Maybe you're throwing away your shot at stardom. But you want to make it big on your own terms, with your own music.

--- THE END ---

To follow another path, turn to page 15.
To learn more about becoming a pop star, turn to page 103.

It may not be superstardom, but it will get your foot in the door of the music industry. You're awestruck when you meet the star you're going to back up. He's warm and friendly. He introduces you to his team of studio musicians and music engineers.

He asks you to sing several songs, and sings along with you for a few of them. Your audition becomes a jam session with his lead vocals and your backup. The star offers you a job as a backup vocalist, and you accept.

His comeback album is a hit, putting the star back on the charts. The press tour for the album is insane. You're flown all over the country to perform on talk shows and do concerts in big cities. That summer, you go on tour. It's amazing!

The star you're backing up gets swarmed by fans everywhere he goes. You feel kind of sorry for him. Nobody recognizes you, though. You're free to go out in public during the day, and spend your nights singing in front of thousands of screaming fans. They're not screaming for you exactly, but you don't care. Who knew being a backup singer would be even more fun than being a star?

--- THE END ---

To follow another path, turn to page 15.
To learn more about becoming a pop star, turn to page 103.

The producers love your song choice. They send you on to the final round. It is the audition in front of the celebrity judges!

The next day, you enter a brightly lit room with the celebrity judges. You spend a moment actually chatting with a star you've loved since childhood. She's so sweet that it calms your nerves. At the last minute, you ditch the pop song you had prepared and perform one you wrote.

You can't hold back the tears as the judges gush about your talent. Your celebrity idol says she'd love to sing one of your songs. They all vote yes. It's unreal. You're going to be on TV! The show sends a TV crew to your hometown. They follow you everywhere. You shoot commercials, interviews, and behind-the-scenes footage. They ask you to sign a lot of legal paperwork, giving away control of your music and management.

A few days before the big LA trip, you get into a car accident that puts you in the hospital. The TV crew films the whole thing. Your doctors urge you to stay home and recover. The producer thinks this "triumph over adversity" story line will make great television. Millions of people will be rooting for you to win.

- To take the doctors' advice and stay home, turn to page 96.
- To go to Los Angeles against your doctors' advice, turn to page 97.

It's a hard blow to get this close to your dreams and have to give up. But your health is more important than stardom. The TV crew packs up and leaves. The producer sends you flowers, and that's the last time you hear from him.

When the cameras are gone you feel like a failure. To your surprise, your old bandmates show up at the hospital. They support you through every step of your recovery. You didn't realize how much you missed them. When you recover, they ask you to rejoin the band. You accept. You'd rather play small shows with true friends than make it big on your own.

--- THE END --

To follow another path, turn to page 15.
To learn more about becoming a pop star, turn to page 103.

Nothing will keep you from your dream. By the time you get to Los Angeles, everyone knows your story.

It's hard work. You keep at it from morning to night, choosing songs, rehearsing, and filming commercials and interviews. You meet with voice coaches and musicians. Every contestant gets money for clothes, so you spend time shopping with a stylist. There's a dress rehearsal at the end of each week—then the live show.

Just like the producer predicted, the whole country is buzzing about your big comeback story. When you hop out onstage on crutches, the crowd goes crazy. You nail your performance and wow the judges. You get voted to go on to the next round! The weeks fly by in a haze until you've made it to the semifinals.

• Turn the page.

By now you're fully healed. The doctor gives you the OK to get rid of the cast and crutches. But the producers say no way! They see your story as a big ratings boost. You're not losing the cast and the crutches until the final show—if you make it.

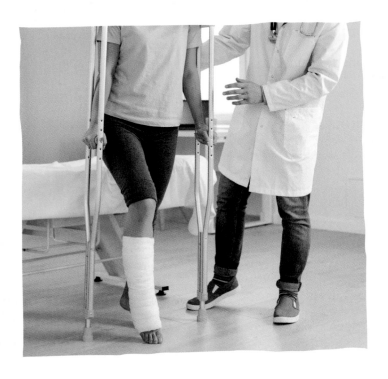

- To keep the cast on, go to page 99.
- To defy the producers, turn to page 100.

You don't like manipulating the audience into feeling sorry for you. But you keep it to yourself as you rehearse for the semifinal round. This week, the celebrity judges choose a contestant to mentor. Your idol chooses you! She wants you to sing an original song. You confide in her about your injury being healed. She reminds you that it's your talent, not your accident, that's going to make you a star.

Performance night arrives. The other contestants are very talented. You feel so guilty about lying about your injury that it's hard for you to concentrate. What if you accidentally put weight on your leg and someone notices? You sing your best, but even the cast isn't enough to save you from losing this round. You break down backstage, knowing how close you got to pop stardom.

--- THE END ---

To follow another path, turn to page 15.
To learn more about becoming a pop star, turn to page 103.

You're not going to be dishonest about yourself, no matter what it costs. The morning of the live show you quietly go to a doctor. She removes the cast and wishes you luck. It's a secret to the judges and producers until the moment you walk out onstage without a cast or crutches, grinning. Everyone gasps in shock. When you're done, the judges jump to their feet, cheering. You make it to the final!

The last week zooms by in a flash. You give dozens of interviews. People from around the country send you truckloads of flowers and gifts.

Finally the big day comes. You belt out one of your original songs, an anthem about power and strength and beating the odds. You'd saved it for this night, if it ever came. The audience goes crazy! You walk off the stage knowing you got this far on your talent.

The other contestant gives a blockbuster performance, and then it's over. The two of you stand on the stage, waiting for the final judgment. When they call your name it takes a few seconds for it to sink in that you've won. You've won! You break down on stage with relief and excitement. Your pop stardom dream has come true!

--- THE END ---

To follow another path, turn to page 15.
To learn more about becoming a pop star, turn to page 103.

THE STRUGGLE FOR STARDOM

Countless artists try to make it big every year. Some go for internet stardom with videos and online concerts. They're encouraged by online stars like The Weeknd and Bad Bunny. Others take the live-performance route. Katy Perry got started singing in church. Ariana Grande began her career by performing in a Broadway musical and on TV. Still others try reality TV. They're inspired by stars like Kelly Clarkson, Carrie Underwood, and Adam Lambert.

Honestly, for most artists, stardom never happens. Fortunately, pop stardom isn't the only job in the music industry. Do you have a way with words? A songwriting career could be for you. Do you enjoy mixing music? Then you might make it as an audio engineer. Do you play an instrument? All pop stars need good studio musicians to play backup on recordings or go on tour. Is organizing your superpower? Then a tour manager, talent buyer, booking agent, music publicist, or artist manager could be the perfect job.

The music industry is constantly changing, and it takes talented, creative people to keep it going. You can build a long and successful career far beyond the bright lights and red carpet.

POP STAR
FAME OR FORTUNE
REALITY CHECK

EDUCATION OR EXPERIENCE

There's no education or experience requirement for pop stardom. Some artists spend decades perfecting their craft. Others make it big before they leave high school. Music or voice lessons never hurt, but they're not necessary. What every pop star must have is talent and the ambition to work for their dream.

SALARY RANGE

The most successful pop stars earn millions of dollars every year. Live performances account for most of their income. They also make money from music sales and merchandise. Less-famous singers average between $45,000 and $65,000 a year.

WHAT THE PROFESSION ENTAILS

Pop stars perform for live audiences, record music, practice singing and dancing, and travel. Some pop stars also play instruments, write songs, appear on television, and act in films.

BEST-KNOWN POP STARS

Drake	Ed Sheeran
Taylor Swift	Justin Bieber
Ariana Grande	Beyoncé
Bad Bunny	Billie Eilish

Ed Sheeran

Beyoncé

OTHER PATHS TO EXPLORE

Many online musicians don't want a record contract. They can make hundreds or thousands of dollars a month with social media, streaming apps, and YouTube channel subscriptions. What are the advantages and disadvantages of a record contract versus a career in online music?

In the past, most reality TV talent shows only allowed unknown, nonprofessional musicians to audition. In recent years, they have been accepting music students and professional artists. Some shows even search the internet to find talented musicians and invite them to audition. The shows argue that they do this to make sure the best talent appears on air. Is it fair for experienced musicians to compete against people who are totally unknown?

GLOSSARY

artist and repertoire (A&R) representative (ARE-tist AND REP-er-twar rep-rih-SEN-tuh-tiv)—a person who finds and recruits new artists for a record label

booking agent (BOOK-ing AYE-juhnt)—a person who arranges live shows and other appearances including television appearances, world tours, and corporate sponsorships

cease and desist letter (SEES AND duh-SIST LE-tuhr)—a document requesting that someone stop doing something that is immoral or illegal and possibly threatening legal action

manager (MAN-uh-juhr)—a person who manages all aspects of a musician's career, negotiating contracts and advising them on professional decisions and business opportunities

music producer (MYOO-zik pruh-DO-ser)—the person responsible for an artist's recording projects

talent buyer (TAH-luhnt BYE-uhr)—the person in charge of finding and booking the musicians for a venue or an event

SELECTED BIBLIOGRAPY

Backup Singers
fastcompany.com/1683210/when-youre-not-the-star-what-you-can-learn-from-the-backup-singers

Bedroom Pop
complex.com/pigeons-and-planes/2018/04/bedroom-pop-diy-artists/clairo

Being a Contestant on American Idol
americanidolnet.com/american-idol-faq/

How to Create a Twitch Music Channel
help.twitch.tv/s/article/twitch-music-fast-start-guide?language=en_US

How to Make Money on YouTube
shopify.com/blog/198134793-how-to-make-money-on-youtube

Making a Demo
recordingconnection.com/reference-library/recording-entrepreneurs/the-best-approach-to-making-a-demo-recording/

Top 10 Music Industry Careers
online.berklee.edu/takenote/top-10-careers-in-the-music-business-and-how-much-money-you-can-make/

What a Music Campaign Looks Like
youtube.com/watch?v=9fAhyaKnyQ4

READ MORE

Nabais, Rita. *The History of Rock: For Big Fans and Little Punks.* Chicago: Triumph Books, 2019.

National Geographic Kids. *Turn It Up!: A Pitch-Perfect History of Music That Rocked the World.* New York: National Geographic Kids, 2019.

Santos, Rita. *Ariana Grande: Pop Star.* New York: Enslow Publishing, 2018.

Schwartz, Heather E. *Beyoncé, the Queen of Pop.* Minneapolis: Lerner Publications, 2018.

INTERNET SITES

Chrome Music Lab
musiclab.chromeexperiments.com

Online Drum Machine
onemotion.com/drum-machine/

Songsmith
songsmith.ms/index.html

Tony B-Machine
tony-b.org/

ABOUT THE AUTHOR

Allison Lassieur has never had pop-star dreams, but she once sang in a choir that went on a multistate tour on the way to Walt Disney World. Today she's an award-winning author of more than 150 history and nonfiction books about everything from Ancient Rome to the International Space Station. Her books have received several Kirkus starred reviews and Booklist recommendations, and her historical novel *Journey to a Promised Land* was awarded the 2020 Kansas Library Association Notable Book Award and Library of Congress Great Reads Book selection. Allison lives in upstate New York with her husband, daughter, a scruffy, lovable mutt named Jingle Jack, and more books than she can count.